Craft Beer

Guide to the Most Popular Craft Beers, Pairing Them with Food, and the History of Microbreweries

Table of Contents

Thank you!

Thank you for buying this book!

If you enjoy the book and get some value from it, I would appreciate if you could **leave an honest review** on the Amazon store after finishing.

Thank you and enjoy the book!

***

Receive updates on new book releases, book promotions and much more from Tadio Diller by signing up to the e-mail list: **http://bit.ly/list_tadiodiller_cs**

***

Follow us, Lean Stone Publishing, the publishing company that published this book. You will receive information on upcoming book launches, free book promotions and much more. Sign up to this e-mail list: **http://bit.ly/list_lsp_cs**

***

Like us at **www.facebook.com/leanstonepublishing**

Follow us on Twitter **@leanstonebooks**

The trademarks that are used are without any consent, and the publication of the trademark is without permission or backing by the trademark owner. All trademarks and brands within this book are for clarifying purposes only and are the owned by the owners themselves, not affiliated with this document.

Introduction

I want to thank you and congratulate you for buying this book, *"Craft Beer - Guide to the Most Popular Craft Beers, Pairing Them with Food, and the History of Microbreweries."*

Have you been drinking the same old beers for years and feel like they have nothing more to offer? There is absolutely nothing wrong with popular beer brands that are circulating in the market these days. In fact, some of them are actually quite nice. However, if you want something different, but still familiar, craft beers may be for you.

Craft beers are those made by independent brewers, or microbreweries, as they like to call themselves. Unlike popular beer brands, most microbreweries can only pump out a couple of crates of their products every day. However, the great thing about craft beers is the care that the brew masters put into making each batch. Yes, craft beers can be a bit more expensive than the ones you usually buy, but once you give them a try, you will find that they are very much worth the extra cost.

In this book, you will learn more about the history of craft beers; how they came about, and how they proliferated all over the country. Additionally, you will also learn about how to pair craft beers with food, just as you would with wine.

I hope that after you finish reading this book, your curiosity about craft beers will be replaced by a strong desire to start collecting and storing them as others do with wine.

Thanks again for buying this book. I hope you enjoy it!

Chapter 1 – What are Craft Beers?

Microbreweries Defined

Strictly defined, microbreweries (those that produce craft beers) are small, independent, and traditional. Microbreweries are small in terms of beer production. Typically, they can only produce 6 million barrels of a product annually and only the larger companies can achieve those kinds of numbers.

Microbreweries can only produce in small quantities because most of them have to follow the rules of *alternating proprietorships*, meaning the "host" brewer needs to rent out their place and equipment to "tenant" brewers; this allows small brewers to make their product and get it out to the market without the need to invest a lot of money.

To be called a microbrewery, it must be run *independently*. This means that no more than 25 percent of company stocks can be under the ownership of a commercial alcoholic beverage maker, unless said company produces craft beers themselves.

Finally, a true microbrewery must use *traditional beer brewing methods*. Craft brewers do not use mainstream brewing equipment and techniques, and most of the time they actually use the techniques used in the early 1900s; some even go as far as using the same equipment, albeit with some modern modifications to make them safer to use. Just like the brewers of old, craft brewers derive the flavor of their beers using different flavoring ingredients in different combinations.

You should not confuse microbreweries with brewpubs. Technically speaking, a brewpub is a bar or restaurant that produces its own beer and serves them right on the premises. In short, all brewpubs are essentially microbreweries, but not all microbreweries are brewpubs.

Why you should Try Craft Beers?

Are you deathly loyal to your favorite big beer brand? Do you really think your favorite is the best one out there? If a beer is your favorite only because you've compared it with other mainstream brands then you are missing out on some delicious libations. To convince you to explore beyond your usual brand, here are some of the more obvious reasons why craft beers are better.

Craft beer isn't a watered down imitation of real beer. One reason to drink beer is to get that nice buzz. You may have noticed that it takes quite a few bottles to give you even the slightest indication of that feeling. If you look at the label of your beer, you will find out that it only contains around 2.5% alcohol by volume (ABV)—lower if you are drinking light beer. Compare that measly ABV to those of craft beers, which usually start at 5-10% ABV and could go as high as a staggering 60% (this is the record held by Snake Venom beer).

You have more choices. If your idea of beer variety is having a choice between Budweiser, Coors, and Miller (of course, this includes the "light" beers), then you are in for a huge surprise. In the United States alone, there are an estimated 1,600 active microbreweries currently making thousands of different beers. There are so many independent small breweries out there that you are probably living within a ten-mile radius of one. Each microbrewery produces its own unique beer and you can taste the difference between each and every one of them.

Craft beers are innovative. Big beer companies are not keen to introduce new products to their lineup. When they discover a formula that sells well, they prefer to stick to it to maximize their profits. Microbreweries, on the other hand, constantly come up with different variations of their products, and they can afford to do so because they can only brew beer in relatively small batches. They can easily recoup their losses should a particular batch not sell as well as they hoped it would.

Some examples of wild, innovative beers that gained huge acclaim are Peanut Butter Cup Porter by Willoughby Brewing Company and Mangalitsa Pig Porter by Right Brain Brewery (yes, this particular beer contains real pork).

Craft beer festivals are the bomb! Forget about snooty, exclusive, and somewhat boring wine tastings. If you want to have a good time while sampling a diverse variety of alcoholic beverages, you should attend at least one craft beer festival each year. Craft beer festivals are held at least monthly across the country. These festivals are great venues to discover new and exciting beers, as well as meet people who share the same interests as you; take this chance to pick the brains of other beer lovers so you can find out just what you have been missing.

You can actually meet the people behind the brews. If you want to meet the owner of Budweiser or of any other big beer companies, odds are you won't even make it past the main door of the company headquarters. This is not the case when it comes to microbreweries. If there is a microbrewery near where you live, then you can actually ask to speak with the owner. You may even get a free tour of the facility if you ask nicely.

Craft beers pair well with different kinds of food. Much like wine, craft beers can actually enhance the flavor of certain foods. Your usual beers may sometimes go well with Buffalo wings, burgers, pizza, even certain steaks, but with the sheer diversity of flavors of craft beers, you can pair them with a wider variety of foods. In fact, many restaurants these days actually offer lists of beers that go well with their entrées.

Drinking craft beers means you support your community. By partaking in craft beers made by local microbreweries, you are also supporting local businesses. More customers drinking local beer mean more employment opportunities and income for your community.

Craft beers taste better. Perhaps the primary reason to try craft beers is that they taste undoubtedly better than the beers you are used to drinking. You may have been drinking the same kind of beer for so long that you actually believe that it's the way real beer should taste, but once a nice bottle of craft beer dampens your lips, you will surely change your opinion. You might not even go back to your old "favorites."

Now that you have figuratively whet your appetite for craft beers, you are ready to learn more about this heavenly libation. The more you learn about craft beer, the more you will appreciate it.

Chapter 2 – A Short History Lesson on Craft Beers, and Why Americans Like Watered Down Beer

We won't be going through the full history of beer in this book because it would take too long to explain. What we will tackle is how the craft brewing industry began in America. In this chapter, you will learn what caused the surge of interest in craft beers and home brewing, and the major players that contributed to the meteoric rise of this relatively new industry.

After Prohibition

The 1910s was a dark age for breweries because this was when the federal government enacted the 18th Amendment to the United States Constitution (also known as Prohibition). This new law made it illegal to brew and sell intoxicating beverages, including beer. However, instead of completely stamping out alcoholic beverages and those who produce them, Prohibition actually caused the number of illegal brewing operations to rise.

The sudden demand for illegal hooch was so tempting that people would willingly risk incarceration just so they could make a nifty profit brewing beer and other alcoholic drinks in their homes.

Besides questionable hygiene, home brewers during the Prohibition era would water down their beer to maximize their profits. Getting the right ingredients for making beer was difficult back then so they had to make do with what they had.

To say that the beer back then was horrible is an understatement; however, people would gladly drink it because they had little choice. After Prohibition was repealed, it seemed that the American brewing industry would make a comeback, but then came the World Wars.

After World War II

The years after World War II saw the rise of the big beer companies. Because they were the ones that provided beer rations to soldiers during the war, these same companies already had an extensive fan base. However, they did not like the beers because of how they tasted, but because they were what they were used to. Thanks to extensive marketing and advertising efforts, the growth of big beer companies continued to grow despite providing substandard products at best.

The growth of big beer seems unstoppable at this point; they even started buying small breweries all over the country, not because of their products, but because of their customer base and distribution systems. The big beer companies did not care for the products of the microbreweries they bought out.

They shut down their production lines and discontinued their products. This practice almost drove American microbreweries into extinction and flooded the market with beer that is but a shadow of its former self. Thankfully, a couple of enterprising people still remembered what real beer tasted like and their undying spirits rekindled the country's passion for brewing beers.

The Rebirth of America's Craft Beer Industry

In 1965, Fritz Maytag, the great-grandson of the Maytag Corporation's Frederick Maytag, heard the news that the Anchor Brewing Company was about to close and he snatched up the opportunity to buy it. Anchor was one of the few remaining independent craft breweries in America at the time and the beers they produced were lackluster at best. Some batches even turned out sour because their equipment was unintentionally contaminated.

Things started to change once Maytag took the reins of the company. He altered their beer recipe and made a couple of improvements to the brewing process and the demand for this new and improved beer started to rise. Anchor Brewing Company rose up from the ashes and became one of the most successful craft brewing companies in the country.

Maytag enjoyed the substantial profits that his company earned and because their operation was small-scale, running the Anchor Brewing Company was relatively stress-free. Unlike big beer companies, Maytag did not want to compromise the quality of their beer by expanding the company and what's more, he actually helped competitor microbreweries become more efficient. This is what rekindled the spark of American craft brewing and made it the billion-dollar industry that it is now.

Modern Craft Breweries

The public interest in home brewing is continuing to rise, and there are no signs of it stopping. Currently, there are more than 3,000 independent craft breweries in America (including brewpubs, microbreweries, and regional craft breweries) and this number is on the rise. People are so interested in brewing their own beers that sales of home brewing kits are skyrocketing.

It seems that the country is finally ending the slump imposed by Prohibition. Craft breweries are cropping up everywhere and now Americans finally have more choices when it comes to their beers. Hopefully, after a couple more years, the global assumption that Americans like watered down beers will begin to change, thanks to the rise of the craft beer brewing industry.

Chapter 3 – Things you Might Not Know About Craft Beers (And Beer in General)

Before we get into the nitty-gritty of craft beers, you should take this opportunity to add a bit of trivia to your knowledge of craft beers. To make things a bit more interesting, here are some things that you might not know about craft beer, and beer in general. These bits of random knowledge may, or may not improve your beer tasting experience, but at least you will have a plethora of interesting subjects to talk about whenever you have a couple of your buddies over for a drink.

1. Despite the reputation for liking watered down beers, American craft beer drinkers actually like drinking India Pale Ale style beers, which happens to be one of the hoppiest beer styles ever made.

2. Male brewers are called "brew masters"; women are called "brewsters."

3. The most popular craft beer style in America also has an interesting origin story. Stories state that English tradesmen were sick and tired of their beer spoiling while shipping it from their mother country to their colonies in India. In an effort to reduce waste (which is a noble endeavor without a doubt), the brewers added more hops to their beers so they could survive the sometimes months-long journey.

   The resulting ale was significantly bitterer than the other beers available back then, but it still had about the same alcohol content. Surprisingly, the stronger-flavored India Pale Ale became a hit for beer drinkers back then, and it is still one of the most popular beer styles today.

4. The most popular kind of hops used in American craft beers is Cascade hops. They are used primarily for their strong aromas. Concerning the flavors Cascade hops give to craft beers, experts say that it provides a citrus-y taste, almost like the taste of a good grapefruit.

5. Speaking of hops, did you know that they come from the same plant family as marijuana? However, don't bother putting hops inside a water pipe and smoking them since they do not smoke well at all.

6. Although most craft beer brewers today are men, back in the day, they would not even be eligible for the job. In ancient Peru, only women from high-ranking families had the right to brew beer.

7. The ancient pyramids may have been paid in part with beer. Some of the wages of the workers who built the ancient monoliths were in the form of beer, and never have you seen happier workers.

8. Archaeologists unearthed ancient Egyptian texts containing more than a hundred medical uses for beer.

9. There is an old Egyptian beer called "bouza" made from fermented millet and is still being brewed in certain areas in Ethiopia. Some linguists have a theory that this may be the origin of the term "booze."

10. Women played a large part in the history of beer. According to legend, they may have been the reason why beer exists. For instance, in Baltic mythology, there is a goddess whose sole purpose is to provide protection for beer. In Finnish folklore, they say that a woman named Kalevatar created beer by mixing honey with bear spit, which seems quite unsavory if you think about it.

11. There was a written law in ancient Egypt that forbade men from brewing beer.

12. Chicha, a traditional Peruvian beer, uses spit as one of its main ingredients.

13. The oldest beer recipe is on a clay tablet dating back to the Sumerians, around 4,000 years ago. However, don't think that it would taste similar to the beers we have today. Besides grains and water, the Sumerians used completely different ingredients.

14. In the Middle Ages, clean drinking water was hard to come by so people were encouraged to drink beer. Back then, animal feces and many other nasty things contaminated most of the water supply.

15. The state with the most craft breweries is California with 330 (and rising), followed by Colorado with 160, Washington with 150, and Oregon with 134.

16. Here's a warning to home brewers who are also pet lovers: hops are poisonous to dogs and cats so keep them away from your brewing operation.

17. Snails and slugs absolutely love the taste of beer. If you are currently dealing with a snail infestation in your garden, leave a shallow container containing beer outside overnight. Come morning, it will be full of these gastropods.

18. Beers are kept in brown bottles to prevent exposure to light because it will cause the beer to spoil faster.

19. Nursing mothers in the 19th century were advised to drink beer, which is a stark contrast to what doctors would tell them nowadays.

20. Since most of the water supply in Medieval England was unsafe to drink, mothers let their young children drink beer as it was much cleaner. Since these kids were still learning to walk and were unaccustomed to the

taste and effects of beer, it would cause them to "toddle" about, which is why we now call young kids "toddlers."

21. Despite numerous health warnings regarding the negative health effects of excessive beer consumption, moderate beer drinking actually has some health benefits. Beer contains a healthy amount of silicon that can help strengthen bones. It also contains dietary fiber that can help maintain your digestive health.

22. In ancient Babylon, it was common practice for the bride's father to provide his new son-in-law with all the mead he could drink for an entire month after the wedding. Mead is a type of honey beer, and since the Babylonians followed a lunar calendar, this period of excessive drinking for the son-in-law was the "honey month," which is supposedly the origin of the modern word "honeymoon."

23. The Code of Hammurabi (the compilation of the laws abided by the ancient Babylonians) states that if a merchant watered down his beer he would be put to death.

24. Another harsh Babylonian law regarding beer stated that if a brewer made a particularly unsatisfactory batch of beer, she (remember that women were the only ones allowed to brew beer back then) would be put to death by drowning in her own product. So, it is safe to assume that the ancient Babylonians really took beer seriously.

25. Here's another connection between beer and weddings: the word "bridal" came from the old tradition of the English wherein men would take their mates out for some "bride ale" the night before their wedding.

26. Back before the invention of the thermometer, brew masters would stick their thumbs into the bunghole of beer barrels to check if their temperatures were just

right, and this is where the phrase "rule of thumb" came from.

27. In 1813, a huge wave of beer flooded the streets of London when a huge vat containing 1.4 million liters of it suddenly ruptured. You might also like to know that the vat was located inside a church (monks back then were avid brewers).

28. The Vikings actually attribute most of their victories to "*aul*," a traditional form of beer that they brewed. In fact, before major battles, the Vikings would down at least a bucket of aul to calm their nerves. Sometimes, the aul worked too well because they would charge into battle without any protective armor. Sometimes they would even forget to wear their shirts, which is why they were called "berserk," an old Scandinavian word meaning "bare chest." The term would eventually evolve to describe their wild form of fighting.

29. Speaking of the Vikings, they believed that when a warrior died on the battlefield it would make him (sometimes her) eligible for passage to Valhalla; once there, they could drink all of the beer they could handle courtesy of a giant goat whose udders contained an unlimited amount of it.

30. The Old Norse word used to describe hangovers is *kveis*, which means "uneasiness after debauchery"; you can be sure that the Vikings used this word quite a lot after every aul-infused battle.

31. Although the modern Catholic Church frowns upon excessive beer drinking, there are actually a few patron saints of brewers.

St. Arnulf of Metz – St. Arnulf is perhaps the most popular of the patron saints of beer. He was once a bishop and royal adviser to the king of Austrasia. A couple of years after his death and after becoming a saint, a couple of his followers travelled a long distance to his grave to exhume and transfer his body to a more suitable location.

The monks underestimated just how far they had to travel and soon found that their supply of beer was starting to get critically low. Being very thirsty and desperate, one of the monks pleaded with St. Arnulf to help them; lo and behold, when they checked their containers their beer supplies were fully replenished thus, enabling them to complete their journey.

St. Augustine – Besides being the patron saint of theologians, printers (the people who run the presses, not the machine connected to your computer), and (strangely enough) sore eyes, St. Augustine also offers his patronage to brewers.

St. Wenceslaus – Although known mostly for his very generous almsgiving and for helping the outcasts of society, St. Wenceslaus is also the patron saint of brewers.

St. Luke the Evangelist – Yes, this is the same St. Luke who wrote the Gospel of Luke in the Bible. St. Luke is the patron saint of many forms of workers, including brewers, the reason for which is still unclear. Some theologians think that this came about because St. Luke was a doctor and he supposedly advocated the drinking of beer because it was cleaner than most of the water available during his time.

32. There are several mentions of beer in the Bible. The most notable passage is *Proverbs 31:6* in the New International Version, *"Give beer to those who are perishing, wine to those who are in anguish."*

[18]

33. Beer also played a part in American history. During the Revolutionary War, Gen. George Washington made it a point that his soldiers get a couple of quarts of beer in their daily rations to keep their morale high. Another interesting fact about Washington: he apparently ran and operated his own brewing operation on his property on Mount Vernon.

34. The Pilgrims apparently wanted to dock the Mayflower a bit further south in warmer climates, but since their beer stores were running low, they had to settle on Plymouth Rock instead.

35. An old English drinking song called the "Anacreon" inspired the music for the Star Spangled Banner.

36. President Theodore Roosevelt, who was probably the manliest of men, once took 500 gallons of beer with him on one of his African safari hunting trips.

37. Besides George Washington, some other US Presidents brewed their own beers. One of them is President Barack Obama who runs and pays out of his own pocket for the operation of a craft brewery inside the White House.

38. In the movie adaptation of the Shawshank Redemption, in the scene where Andy and Red drink beers on the roof of the prison warden, the filmmakers actually got their period beer container wrong. In the movie, they drink Stroh's Bohemian Style Beer; however, the label on the bottles was the one the company used in *1950*. The movie was set in *1949*.

39. England's King Henry VIII once condemned the use of hops in flavoring beer. He actually said that hops were a "wicked and pernicious weed" that does nothing but ruin the flavor of beer.

40. Hops serve two purposes in beer making. One is that it offsets the sweetness from the sugars produced by the fermentation of the grains. The second job is that it serves as a preservative to prolong the shelf life of beer.

41. Porter beers first became popular during the Industrial Revolution, and at the time, they weren't called porters at all. The name came about because this was the style of beer popular with dockworkers, also known as *"porters."*

42. Apparently, you can use beer as hair conditioner. If you use (good quality) beer on your hair after shampooing, it will leave it smooth and shiny.

43. During Oktoberfest, an estimated 7.1 million liters of beer will be served to thirsty patrons. That volume is enough to fill three Olympic-size swimming pools.

44. A beer's color depends on how much malt it contains; the higher the malt content, the darker and sweeter the beer.

45. The most expensive craft beer in the world is Vielle bon Secours. It costs around $1,000 a bottle and you can only buy it at one bar, the Bierdrome in London.

46. Beer can make you smarter (if you are a woman). Studies show that women who drink moderate amounts of beer had better cognitive functions in comparison to non-drinkers.

47. Lambic beer is the only beer style that still uses the same kind of wild yeast that the very first beer brewers used. Modern Lambic brewers use a particularly strong type of yeast that occurs in the village of Lembeeck in Belgium, which also gave it its name.

48. The beer equivalent of the wine sommelier is the cicerone. There are three levels of beer masters:

Certified Beer Server, Certified Cicerone, and Certified Master Cicerone. If you want to become a cicerone, you have to take a written and practical test.

49. Since the program started in 2008, only four Americans have earned the title of Certified Master Cicerone, and one of them is a woman.

50. People have risked their lives to save beer. In 2001, a truck in Australia carrying a large shipment of beer blew a tire and ended up sinking in a river; the driver was lucky enough to escape. In no time at all, locals started swarming the accident area, some of them donning full scuba gear, in an attempt to salvage as much of the stuff as they could. One man apparently made away with 400 bottles. Of course, none of the beer found its way back to the company.

These are just some of the many interesting facts surrounding everyone's favorite alcoholic drink. The sheer amount of things like these just proves the point that beer has undoubtedly left an indelible mark on human civilization, and as long as people are still brewing it, there is little doubt that it will continue influencing the course of history.

Chapter 4 – Notable Craft Breweries and Why You Should Give Them a Try

It was mentioned earlier that there are hundreds, if not thousands, of craft breweries in the United States. However, not all of them produce good beer. Some make beers that are so-so at best, while some produce horrible brews. In this chapter, you will learn about the companies whose beers are top-notch. If you want to be a true beer connoisseur, take note of these and make it a point to try every one of them.

In no particular order, here are some of the best craft breweries in the US right now:

Allagash Brewing Company (Portland, Maine)

Allagash Brewing Company was founded in 1995 and began as a one-man operation by the founder and owner Rob Tod. Tod worked in a brewery before, and he noticed that there was a considerable void in the craft brewing industry: there were not enough Belgian-style beers on the market. To take advantage of this market void, Tod designed his first brew house, a small 15-barrel operation and started making traditional Belgian-style beer.

In the summer of 1995, Tod sold his first case of beer and people were immediately hooked. Today, Allagash produces six different kinds of beer, not including the special beers that they produce only once a year and the one-off beers that they produce for special occasions.

The best beer they have is *Curieux*, a Belgian tripel that they allowed to age in old Jim Beam barrels. This results to the beer having a slight vanilla taste and a hint of bourbon. Curieux costs around $20 per 750ml bottle and has 11 percent ABV.

Brewery Ommegang (Cooperstown, New York)

Cooperstown was, and still is, a baseball-crazy town, but in 1997, it also became a beer-crazy town when Brewery Ommegang was established. Built on 136 acres that used to be a hop farm (the perfect place for a brew house), Ommegang became the first ever homestead brewery in the US in the last 100 years. Its focus is on making Belgian-style ales and it currently produces 7 different kinds on a regular basis.

Ommegang has actually become so popular that HBO collaborated with the brewery to produce a limited edition beer for the premiere of the fifth season of *Game of Thrones*: a Dark Saison ale aptly named *The Three-eyed Raven*.

However, the Three-eyed Raven is not Ommegang's bestseller; that distinction falls on *The Three Philosophers*, a perfect combination of Belgian Quadrupel and Kriek. The Three Philosophers has a sweet, malty flavor, with a subtle stone fruit undertone. Its unique flavor profile makes it perfect for pairing with desserts. The Three Philosophers sells for around $9 per 750ml bottle and contains 9.7 percent ABV.

Anchor Brewing Company (San Francisco, California)

You cannot make a list of the best craft beer breweries in America without mentioning the one that started it all. Anchor Brewing Company got its start when German immigrant Ernst Baruth and his son-in-law, Otto Schinkel Jr. bought an old, Gold Rush era brewery and started German-style beers. A series of unfortunate events (including the deaths of both founders and the advent of Prohibition) caused the company to teeter close to bankruptcy.

The company went through several different management changes throughout the years, but it was only when Fritz Maytag bought the company and instilled major changes in operations and production that the Anchor Brewing Company became a frontrunner in the craft beer industry.

Anchor's signature beer, and the one that they have been producing ever since the company began, is the Steam Beer, however, beer lovers agree that their *Old Foghorn ale* is the best. Old Foghorn uses almost three times the amount of malt used in most other craft beers, but it still attains a perfect balance of sweetness and fruitiness, thanks to their use of traditional English barley wine brewing methods. Old Foghorn sells for around $15 for a six-pack of 12 oz. bottles, and it contains 8.2 percent ABV.

Sierra Nevada (Chico, California)

The Sierra Nevada brewing company started back in the 1970s when Ken Grossman and Paul Camusi started brewing the kind of beer they'd want to drink. Back then, it was difficult to obtain hops for their home brewing operation, and many of the ones that were available were not that good at all. This forced Grossman to travel all the way to Washington State from California so he could convince hop growers to sell directly to him.

He asked the growers if he could have some "brewer's cuts," which were essentially product samples, so he could find which ones worked with his beer. This is when he discovered how to use whole cone hops to create the kind of hop-forward beer for which his company is now famous.

The very first beer that ever came out of the Sierra Nevada brewery is their famous *Pale Ale*. Grossman almost went bankrupt in his quest to find the perfect recipe for it. He dumped ten whole batches of beer because he felt that they are not what he wanted. After extensive trial and error, Grossman finally found the right recipe and the rest is history.

Because they use only fresh and full-cone hops, the Sierra Nevada Pale Ale offers a very fragrant bouquet, which is also the reason for its rather spicy and citrusy flavor. Since it has a relatively low ABV (5.6 percent) and it is cheaper than most other craft beers (at $9 for a six-pack of 12oz bottles), many consider their Pale Ale as the ideal *"gateway beer"* for budding beer enthusiasts.

Three Floyds Brewing Company (Munster, Indiana)

Brothers Nick and Simon, and their father, Mike Floyd, founded the Three Floyds Brewing Company. The company's home was once a rundown warehouse, until the Floyds got their hands on it. They transformed the once dank building into a full-blown brewery where they create concoctions that they say are *"normal"* by craft beer standards. Thanks to their unusual, yet very delicious beers, the Three Floyds Brewing Company gathered probably the most fanatical customer base among all the craft brewers out there.

Their most popular beer is the *Dark Lord*, a Russian Imperial stout that contains coffee, vanilla, and sugar, which gives the beer an unapologetically intense malt flavor and extremely dark color, rather high ABV (15%), and unusual texture. Even though it may look menacing, it is actually one of the best craft beers available. If you want to get your hands on this unusual beer, you need to prepare your wallet and mark your calendars. The Dark Lord is only available for one day every April in the brewery and will set you back around $60 for a 4-pack of 20oz bottles.

Cigar City Brewing Company (Tampa, Florida)

According to the owners, there are two reasons why the Cigar City Brewing Company came into being: first is so they can share the colorful culture of Cigar City with the world, and second is so they can make the best beer in the world; and it seems like they are actually making good on their promises. Cigar City has an unusual lineup of craft beers, which says a lot because craft beer companies are notorious for their bizarre offerings.

One of the most popular beers to have ever come out of the Cigar City brewery is *Good Gourd*, a beer flavored with pumpkin spice and other spices that you would normally expect in a pumpkin pie, not a beer. Good Gourd is a seasonal offering; the brewery only sells it during the fall season, often coinciding with Thanksgiving. Good Gourd has a respectable 8.5 percent ABV, making it the perfect pairing for most of the food found on a Thanksgiving table.

Maine Beer Company (Freeport, Maine)

The Maine Beer Company started when two brothers, Dave and Daniel Kleban, decided to drive three hours both ways to get a home brewing kit that they saw on Craigslist. Though it started as a hobby, it became a full-blown business. However, even though the company has grown, they still hung onto their desire to remain a family business, and the moral stance that they will always "do what's right" by giving 1% of their profits to environmental organizations.

Maine Beer Company does not concentrate on making one style of beer, and their rate of production is somewhat slow because all of their beers are bottle-conditioned, but one thing is for certain: all of their beers are made with love and care. Take their bestseller *Lunch,* for instance, which is what they call an "East Coast version" of the West Coast style IPA, but unlike their counterpart, Lunch has a more intense hops flavor and the aroma of tropical fruits and pine.

Victory Brewing Company (Downingtown, Pennsylvania)

Best friends Bill Covaleski and Ron Barchet created one of the oldest craft breweries in the US, Victory Brewing Company, way back in 1996. During their first year of operation, they struggled to produce 1,700 barrels of beer, but now, thanks to their more modern facilities and experienced staff, their production numbers have risen exponentially. Victory is one of the very few American craft breweries that uses whole hops to flavor their beers. They insist that this gives the final product a more robust flavor and aroma.

[26]

One of their more popular offerings, the seasonal *Summer Love*, a blonde American ale with a 5.7 percent ABV, has a distinct fruity aftertaste, thanks to the use of whole hops.

D.G. Yuengling & Son (Pottsville, Pennsylvania)

The oldest, still operational brewery in America, Yuengling continues to produce beer that has strength and pride, symbolized by the American eagle on their logo. What's surprising is that even after more than a hundred years in operation, the Yuengling family still owns and manages the company. Yuengling & Son is one of the few breweries that actually survived through Prohibition, which they did by brewing "near beers," concoctions that have no more than 0.5 percent ABV.

After Prohibition, the brewery started making its now iconic Winner beer, which they shipped a truckload of to the White House to show President Roosevelt their appreciation. Yuengling currently produces seven different kinds of beer (including a not-so-popular Light beer) and among them, it is the *Traditional Lager* that has become the company's signature offering. It has become so popular in the Pennsylvania area that you can actually get it just by asking for a lager.

Although it has a lower ABV than most other craft beers (4.4 percent), it has a flavor combination of cluster and cascade hops along with roasted caramel malt that makes the people come back for more.

Bell's Brewery Incorporated (Galesburg, Michigan)

When Larry Bell (founder and owner of Bell's Brewery) started making beer, he did not have any fancy equipment; he made beer using a 15-gallon soup kettle. From its humble beginnings, the company now operates out of a 130,000 square foot building built on 32 acres of land. With more than

[27]

20 offerings, Bell's has one of the largest beer catalogs of all the craft breweries in the country.

Out of all the beers that Bell's produces, *Oberon* put the brewery on the map. Oberon uses an eclectic mix of ingredients that gives it a spicy and slightly fruity flavor, as well as wheat malt making the beer pleasantly smooth and easy to drink, which is why many consider it as the perfect summer beer.

Deschutes Brewery (Bend, Oregon)

When Danny Fish established the Deschutes Brewery back in 1988, it was only a small brewpub (a pub that brews their own beer), and he wanted the people in the community to feel like it was *"theirs."* However, after a couple of years, more and more people from outside the local community started discovering their masterfully created brews. When the demand grew to more than what their small operation can handle, they moved into a bigger building that enabled them to increase production exponentially.

Of all their beers, *Freshly Squeezed IPA* (6 percent ABV) has the most solid following. Deschutes crafted this beer by carefully balancing three different kinds of malts and three different of hops, which resulted to an IPA that has a rather strong citrus flavor that some say reminds them of fresh grapefruits. Freshly Squeezed was once only available in the Deschutes brewpub, but thanks to their recent expansion, this IPA is now available in 28 states. Freshly Squeezed costs around $6 per 22oz bottle. Since it is a seasonal beer, it is only available from June until September.

Goose Island Brewery (Chicago, Illinois)

It all started when the founder John Hall went on a beer tasting tour all over Europe. In the middle of his trip, he came to the realization that it is not fair that most Americans could not experience the kind of high quality beer that Europeans

[28]

enjoy. Upon his return to the States in '88, Hall settled in his hometown of Chicago and established the Goose Island Brewery.

Back then, craft brewing was still in its infancy, so to beef up his consumer base, besides making excellent beer, he also invited people to tour the brewery so they knew how their beer was made. This move proved to be successful since the company has been constantly growing and expanding since.

If you have to choose just one of their many beer offerings then you should pick the *Goose Island Bourbon County Stout*. This is a dense and extremely dark barrel-aged stout that has more flavor in one bottle than in an entire case of other beers. You need to be careful not to get too carried away with all of the luscious flavors that the Bourbon County has, for it has a 14 percent ABV.

Goose Island only releases the Bourbon County once a year (because it needs to develop in the bottle for five years) so you need to be on your toes and snatch up a bottle once they are available.

Hill Farmstead (North Greensboro, Vermont)

This brewery epitomizes the real essence of craft beer. They produce beer in small batches, and do not cut corners when it comes to quality. They will make you work hard to get a bottle of their fine brews. Owner and proprietor Shaun Hill built his modest-sized brewery (with plans for future expansion) on his grandfather's dairy farm. He got the idea to brew his own beer after many years of traveling and sampling different kinds of beer from all over the world.

It may seem cruel, but Hill is adamant about keeping the production of his beers relatively low to prevent any decline in quality. As such, you can only get them in the brewery and in around 20 different bars all over Vermont. If you are lucky and you find yourself in New York or Philadelphia during the few times a year when Hill Farmstead sends a couple of cases of beer to their distributors, then you might stand a chance of getting your hands on their exceptional brews.

One of their rarest and most sought after beers is the *Sue*, a variant of their other beer, the *Susan*. This beer is fermented using wild yeast and left to age for a year in French oak barrels, resulting in a libation that is slightly tart and has a delicate hoppy flavor. If you are lucky enough to time your trip to Vermont just right, you can get a 750ml bottle of Sue for $25 and forget about hoarding it as Hill Farmstead only allows a maximum of four bottles per person.

Russian River Brewing Company (Santa Rosa, California)

The company was originally owned by the Korbel Champagne Cellars and founded on their own vineyards in Guerneville, California, near the banks of the beautiful Russian River, which is where the company got its name. In 2003, Korbel decided to get out of the craft beer business and sold the rights to the brand and company to the current owners, husband and wife team Vinnie and Natalie Cilurzo.

When the Cilurzos reopened the company as a brewpub in downtown Santa Rosa, the demand for their carefully crafted beers had gotten so high that they had to open a separate brewery just a mile away to keep up with the demand. Currently, the demand is still higher than their rate of production, but the Cilurzos said that they have no further plans for expansion in fear that by doing so, they will compromise the quality of their products too much.

One of their most famous brews is the *Supplication*, a brown ale that RRBC allows to age in Pinot Noir barrels that the company procures from nearby Sonoma County wineries. Barrel aging imparts a slightly tart flavor to the beer with a dry finish that is similar to the kind you get after sipping fine wine.

Like drinking wine, it is advisable that you let this beer open up a bit after pouring it.

Dogfish Head (Milton, Delaware)

In the industry for more than twenty years, Dogfish Head is possibly the most popular craft beer brewery in the US. When Sam Calagione first opened Dogfish Head in 1995, it was the first brewpub in all of Delaware and was the smallest commercial brewery in the country. Now, however, they operate inside a 100,000 square foot converted cannery that enables them to produce an enormous amount of craft beer, and they have an extensive distribution network that lets people from 28 different states get a taste of their famous concoctions.

In the true spirit of craft brewing, Sam Calagione is not afraid of shaking things up when it comes to beer, thus earning him the distinction of being the most innovative craft brewer in the US.

Among their wide range of beer offerings, Dogfish Head is particularly proud of the *World Wide Stout*. This fine ale is brewed using an enormous amount of barley and a blend of different kinds of hops, giving it a refined taste and depth that is more reminiscent of good port wine than a can of mainstream beer. Be careful though that you do not get carried away too much with its deliciousness for World Wide Stout has a staggering 15-20 percent ABV.

These are only a few of the great craft beer breweries that are currently operating in the US. There are surely other great companies producing great beers, but there is only so much space in this book, and it would be impossible to name them all. For now, the ones in this list can serve as your beginner's introduction to the world of craft beer and after some time has passed, you will be able to discover more great breweries on your own.

Chapter 5 – Pairing Craft Beer with Food

This might ruffle some wine connoisseurs' feathers, but craft beer is actually better for pairing with food than wine. This is because most red wines taste the same as other red wines, the same goes with white wines. Beer is, however, a different story. There are many different kinds of beer and the craft brewers have their own version of them.

However, even though a wider variety of flavors means you have more choices when it comes to food pairings, it also makes it a bit trickier since there are many more things that you have to consider. This chapter will give you the lowdown on beer and food pairing to give you a jumpstart on the subject and push you in the right direction.

Use Your Senses to Your Advantage

Since beer-food pairing is usually subjective, it would be best to actually know your beer thoroughly by sampling it yourself rather than basing all your decisions on a guide that someone else made. First, pour your beer in a glass, let it air out a bit then take a couple of sniffs. Your nose is actually better at picking out individual flavor components than your tongue, which is quite weird, I know. After getting a whiff, what are the things that you smell? Is there are fruity smell in there? Something smoky? Are you getting herbs? Take note of the things that you smell. You will need them later.

After sniffing the beer, take a couple of sips and coat the entire inside of your mouth with it. Are the tastes you're getting in line with the aromas you picked up before? Did an unexpected flavor surprise you? Finally, take note of how the beer felt when you took a sip; consider the beer's carbonation and if it feels full-bodied or not.

Find the Common Ground between the Beer and Food

Pairing craft beer with food is all about the flavors complementing each other, so you need to find foods that taste similar to the beer you plan to drink. For instance, most stout beers have a slightly bitter chocolate aftertaste; naturally, it would go well with desserts and some savory dishes that contain chocolate.

On the other hand, West Coast pale ales have a slight citrus flavor, so you cannot go wrong pairing them with Mexican dishes, most notably salsas and ceviche, or anything that contains a good amount of lime juice. Another beer that goes well with most foods is the porter. These beers have a slightly caramel-like taste, which makes them perfect for barbecues and anything with caramelized onions.

Delicate with Delicate; Bold with Bold

It cannot be stressed enough that the reason for pairing food with beer is so the two can work together and enhance each other's flavors. Naturally, trying to pair bold-flavored foods with a mild-flavored beer is completely wrong.

A good indicator of the intensity of the flavor of a particular beer is its alcohol content. Typically, the higher the ABV, the more intense its flavor will be. For instance, Dogfish Head's World Wide Stout has an ABV of 15 to 20 percent, which is on the upper portion of the beer spectrum. This means that it can go well with similarly strong flavored food, like chili or a Chicago-style deep dish pizza. On the other hand, Sierra Nevada Pale Ale with its relatively low ABV (5 percent) makes it great for delicate fare like Greek salad and fish dishes.

Make Use of the Effervescence

One of the biggest advantages that beer has over wine is its effervescence, otherwise known as the beer bubbles. The bubbles from the beer are great for cleaning the palate,

[33]

thereby ensuring that each bite of food will have as much flavor as the last.

This works well when you plan to dine on fatty or oily foods that have a tendency to coat your palate. For instance, if you want to enjoy every morsel on your cheese platter, pair it with a beer that has a high carbonation like German Hefeweizen.

To make it a bit easier for a novice like yourself, here is a small cheat sheet on pairing food with a particular style of beer that you can use while you are still learning the ropes:

Steaks go well with *Porters*

Salads go well with *Hefeweizen*

Seafood goes well with *Witbier*

Burgers go well with *Brown Ale*

Caribbean Herbed Chicken goes well with *Saison*

Chocolate goes well with *Imperial Stout*

Mexican Food goes well with *Pale Ale*

Pork goes well with *English Bitter*

With these tips in mind, you are well on your way to becoming a real beer connoisseur. Keep in mind that you should not base all of your decisions on the contents of this chapter. As explained, beer tasting is subjective. What one person tastes in beer may not be the same as another's palate. Be adventurous, try different food and beer combinations and find which ones work for you.

***

Receive e-mail updates on new book releases and free book promotions from Tadio Diller. By visiting the link below

http://bit.ly/list_tadiodiller_cs

***

Conclusion

Thank you again for downloading this book!

I hope it was able to help you to gain a deeper understanding and appreciation for craft beer and all the work that the brewers go through for you to enjoy them.

The next step is to take what you learned from this book and apply it as best as you can. You should also not limit yourself to just the contents of this book. There are many other sources of craft beer information out there, and it would do you good to expand your knowledge and continuously improve upon your craft.

Go out there and look for as many craft breweries as you can and sample their wares. There is no guarantee that every craft beer you try will blow your mind, but one thing is for sure, they will be a whole lot better than the watered down excuses for beer that you have in your fridge right now.

Finally, if you enjoyed this book, then I'd like to ask you for a favor. Would you be kind enough to leave a review for this book on Amazon? It'd be greatly appreciated!

Thank you and good luck!

***

Receive e-mail updates on new book releases and free book promotions from Tadio Diller. By visiting the link below

http://bit.ly/list_tadiodiller_cs

***

Check Out My Other Books!

You will find these books by simply searching for them on Amazon.com

This book will show you everything you ever wanted to know about beer from its history to how to find the perfect beer for any meal. It will introduce you to new beers and help you explore beers beyond the common big commercial light beers.

The book shows you how to make sure your next party is unforgettable. With the tips and recipes in this book you will be able to make all of your favorite cocktails right in your own home.

For too many people wine can be a little intimidating. You may know you love the taste of a red or a white wine, but how do you know what kind of wine to order at a restaurant? How can you choose the right wine for your dinner party when there are so many options?

This easy to follow guide will show you how to host a prim and proper afternoon tea, just like the English have been enjoying for generations. If you have watched *Dowton Abbey* and wanted to make afternoon tea part of your routine or even just wanted to host an afternoon tea for a special occasion, this is the book for you.

Tea is the most popular drink in the world. Not even the biggest soda companies in the world can match the number of dedicated drinkers tea boasts. From China to England, tea is seen as a delicious and relaxing drink.

A single cup of delicious, life affirming coffee can set you back two bucks or more at your local coffee shop. Did you know you can make coffee at home that not only costs much less, but actually tastes even better than what you are getting at the coffee shop?

Greetings from the Lean Stone Publishing Company

We want to thank you so much for reading this book to the end. We are committed to creating life changing books in the Self Help area, such as this one that you just read.

If you liked this book and want to follow us for more information on upcoming book launches, free promotions and special offers, then follow us on Facebook and Twitter!

Sign up for e-mail updates on new releases and free promotions by visiting this link:

http://bit.ly/list_lsp_cs

Like us: **www.facebook.com/leanstonepublishing**

Follow: **@leanstonebooks**

Thank you again for reading to the end, it means the world to us!

Printed in Great Britain
by Amazon

43961942R00025